Peter Riley

ESHOLT
A Bygone Era

P & D Riley

First published 2008

P & D Riley
12 Bridgeway East
Cheshire
WA7 6LD
England

e-mail: pdriley@ntlworld.com
website: www.pdriley.co.uk

ISBN: 978 1 874712 80 0

British Library Cataloguing in Publication Data
A catalogue record for this book is available from the British Library

Printed in England

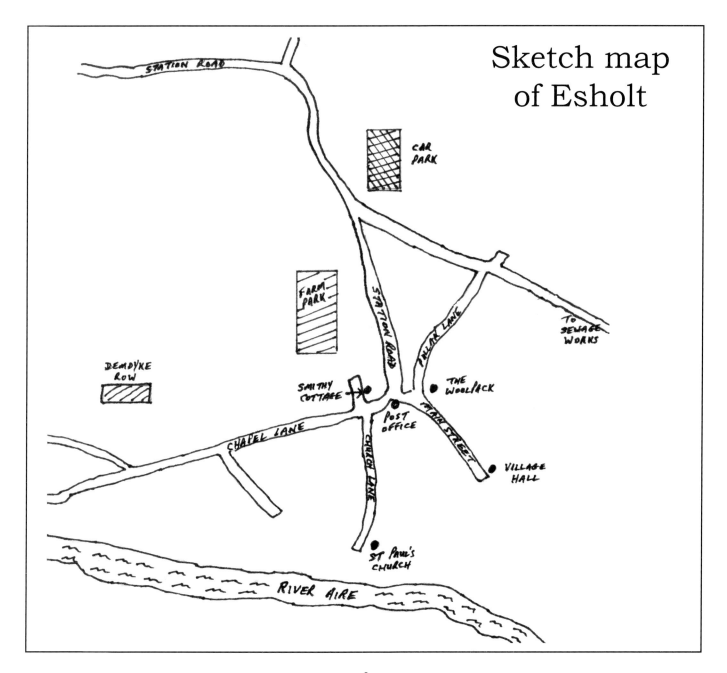

Sketch map
of Esholt

Acknowledgements

The author would like to thank the following for their help in the preparation of this book

Staff in the Local Studies Unit of Bradford Library for their courtesy and
tremendous help in finding newspaper cuttings, out of print books and photographs

Leeds Library & Information Service

John Goude, Manager of Esholt Hall Conference Centre for permission
to take photographs inside Esholt Hall

Paul Garner of Esholt Hall Conference Centre for supplying information

Nicki and Richard McGrath of The Woolpack, Esholt

Ian French of Esholt Post Office

The Bank of England Museum

Mark Morton for permission to use his photograph of Esholt Water Treatment Works

ITV Granada

By the same author:

The Highways and Byways of Sherlock Holmes; The Highways and Byways of Jack the Ripper;
Wythenshawe Hall and the Tatton Family; Heaton Hall and the Egerton Family;
Haigh Hall and the Bradshaigh Family; Bramall Hall and the Davenport Family;
Crewe Hall and The Crewe Family; Manchester Then and Now; Pits and Looms; Warrington Then and Now; Leigh
Then and Now; A Short History of Culcheth (with Oscar Plant); Leigh, Tyldesley and Atherton A Bygone Era; Newton-
le-Willows A Bygone Era; The World of Crime (with Mark Llewellin);
Wythenshawe A Bygone Era (with Susan Hall); A History of Peel Hall; Place to Place; Manchester As It Is;
Holmfirth A Bygone Era; Chester A Bygone Era; The Highways & Byways of Charles Dickens

Early days

The rural tranquillity of Esholt village and surrounding district is like an oasis in the otherwise hectic world of the 21st century, and we can be forgiven for thinking we have been transported back to the days of 'Merrie England' as we look at the lovely cottages, tiny village church, old school house, inn, woodland and pleasant fields. The village is also an extremely proud place, with cottage owners providing a blaze of colour from the hanging baskets and gardens full of plants in bloom during the spring and summer months.

It is a village built of beautiful, sturdy Yorkshire stone which has weathered naturally and magnificently, unlike other parts of the county where stone has aged prematurely through pollution. In Esholt it has retained a yellowish, sandy colour that looks as though it could stand for a thousand years.

According to most local historians Esholt takes its name from *Esche* or Ash and *Holt* or wood, in other words 'Ash Wood' which is logical since so much of the area around the village is still heavily wooded to this day. When the name was first mooted about the time of William the Conqueror the area, like much of England, would have been heavily forested.

It was the coming of a Cistercian order of nuns in 1172 that we can guess was the start of the fortunes of the district and in that year it was recorded that Esche-holt in Airedale was given to the nuns of Sinningthwaite, near Wetherby by Alexander III. The nuns, from the Cistercian Order at Fountains Abbey and Kirkstall Abbey, founded a nunnery in Esholt that relied on the goodwill of local people, in particular the families of Ward, Plumpton and Calverley.

The Esholt priory only lasted until 1540 when the dissolution of the monasteries was ordered by Henry VIII and it became Crown property for the next few years before the king gave it to Henry Thompson of Dover, one of his gentlemen-at-arms who had impressed him by his actions in the siege of Boulogne.

The king's 'generosity' meant Thompson came into possession of substantial holdings in Yorkshire, though he didn't take actual possession until two years after the death of Henry VIII due to a complicated legal structure which had meant Thompson giving up his property in Dover and paying a fee of £555.6s.8d (£555.32p), a huge amount in those days. In a type of Tudor red-tape, which still exists to this day in legal matters, Thompson had paid the cash and surrendered his Dover holdings in December

1544 but didn't get the official stamp of approval in a Letters Patent until July 1547, seven months after the king's death, but it was a further two years before he actually took possession of Esholt and land in Cumberland.

The Thompson family retained ownership of the Esholt estate for more than a century and in 1662 Henry Thompson's grandson, also called Henry, left the land to his only daughter Frances who married Sir Walter Calverley of Calverley Old Hall.

It was the son of Frances and Sir Walter, also called Walter, who eventually succeeded to the Esholt estate and who eventually decided that the ancient pile of Calverley Old Hall wasn't suitable or modern enough any longer, and he commissioned the building of present Esholt Hall. The hall took three years to build, between 1706 and 1709, and during its construction he married Julia Blackett, the daughter of Sir William Blackett, on January 7, 1707. Four years later Walter's fortunes and influence increased dramatically when he was made a baronet in 1711.

The new hall, a splendid building, was constructed on the site of the house built by Henry Thompson and it offered magnificent views over countryside and the River Aire.

The son of Walter and Julia, also named Walter, went one step further and adopted the surname Blackett, thus effectively ending the Calverley connection to the estate. The final connection of all came in 1755 when Walter sold the property to Robert Stansfield, a Bradford drysalter, for the princely sum of £40,000 (the equivalent today of £3,771,200). With such a large sum offered it is not surprising that it was too good to be refused. It also offers a fascinating insight into the great personal wealth of many British industrialists in the 18th century.

Robert Stansfield expanded the Esholt estate and had a gatehouse built in Apperley Lane which later was converted into a public house called the Stansfield Arms, which still exists. The Stansfield family lived in Esholt Hall for 150 years until 1906 when they sold the house and estate to Bradford Corporation for a mere £250,000.

Esholt was built as a village for local workers on the estate and was typical of hundreds of such rural communities that existed until the Second World War as isolated, almost self-contained communities, that were idyllic in appearance if not necessarily in the way people lived.

Like its peers elsewhere in Yorkshire , Esholt once boasted of its own busy little industries and the village had its own blacksmith shop, owned for most of the 19th century by the Nunwich family, a tannery and a mill. Most of the lovely cottages were for use by workers in these local businesses. Some of the properties were also used to house labourers and craftsmen who were forced to live in the village during construction of the railway which was built across the valley between Ilkley and Skipton in the Victorian era.

As with any community in Britain, an inn was considered as essential for the recreation of the local community, and with the growth of such industries as the village mill and tannery it soon became neces-

The Stansfield Arms as it now looks

sary for one to be provided. Today, thanks to the Esholt connection with the TV series *Emmerdale* (previously *Emmerdale Farm*) the village pub is called the Woolpack, a much more rural sounding name than The Commercial Inn that it was before the programme dropped in for many years using it as a location. In a previous existence, almost two centuries ago, the inn was called The Combers Arms, a reminder of the textile industry which played such a major part in promoting this part of Yorkshire.

Another requirement of any village life was (and remains) a church, and in this respect too Esholt was no different to other communities. The village gained its own place of worship in 1842 when St Paul's was built by William Crompton Stansfield. Today the church attracts visitors from all the world thanks to the lingering spirit of Emmerdale, and its visitors book reflects the opinions of many that St Paul's is an oasis of peace and quiet in an otherwise stressed out world.

St Paul's is also the final resting place for members of the Stansfield family, including its patron, William, who also played a very important part in helping Esholt to keep its rural beauty by vigorously opposing any plans to bring more industrial investment to the village in addition to the two textile mills that already operated in the area during his tenure as unofficial 'Lord of the Manor'. His concern for the welfare of Esholt was later inherited by his three daughters and a nephew who continued the tradition of maintaining the rural status-quo.

Left: Sir Walter Calverley who married
Julia Blackett

Right: Lady Julia Calverley, nee Blackett

Below: Sir Walter Calverley- Blackett,
son of Sir Walter and Lady Julia, who
sold Esholt Hall

Esholt Old Hall

Esholt Old Hall in the centre of the village dates to the late 16th century though with late additions built in the mid-17th century by the Calverley family.

The present building, a solid two-storey structure of large coursed gritstone blocks and stone slate roof, stands on the site of a much earlier building which historians believe dates back to the 14th century and the time of the nunnery.

Records show that the hall, which was built around a 15th century open hall, complete with upright and horizontal timbers and oak panelling, was once surrounded by a moat and a large ditch which ran from the west to the south of the property may have been remains of this defensive waterway.

The original hall once belonged to Sir Richard Shireburn (1526-94) who had bought the west sector of the Esholt manor from Sir John Constable in 1567.

Sir Richard was a man of great wealth and influence, a Roman Catholic who was descended from a long line of land owners, and who was, at the time of the purchase of Esholt Old Hall, also overseeing the building of the family seat at Stoneyhurst in Lancashire (now the famous Stoneyhurst Catholic College). He married Alice the daughter of William de Plumpton, another landowner, and it is believed that the couple moved into Esholt Old Hall for a time, particularly as it has been documented that Sir Richard owned several iron smelting works in the woodlands around Esholt, though to date nobody has found any archaelogical evidence on where they were sited.

Sir Richard died in 1594 and was buried in Mitton, Lancashire. Within All Hallows Church in Mitton a monument to Sir Richard and other members of his family can be found to this day inside the aptly named Shireburn Chapel which dates back to 1440 but was rebuilt after Sir Richard's death.

A century after the death of Sir Richard his grandson, Sir Nicholas Shireburn, left Esholt Old Hall to live at Stoneyhurst, and on his death in 1717 the hall came into the possession of his daughter Mary Maria Winifred Francisca, Duchess of Norfolk, who, in 1709, had married Thomas Howard, the 8th Duke of Norfolk of Arundel Castle in Sussex further expanding the family fortunes.

Today Esholt Old hall is a Grade II listed building which gives it protection from destruction or major alterations and is therefore preserved for future generations to enjoy.

An old picture postcard of Esholt Hall from a
watercolour painting around the turn of the 20th century

Esholt Old Hall as it looks today

The Overseers of Esholt

The appearance of Esholt today is one of contentment and prosperity with its chocolate box houses and cottages, but this was not always the case. Indeed records show that many villagers were desperately poor and were forced to appeal for help from the parish. Luckily successive governments had established a series of poor relief laws that provided for parishes to relieve its elderly and helpless citizens and to "bring up unprotected children in 'habits of industry', and provide work for the able-bodied who could not work in their usual trade."

The responsibility of doling out help in whatever form was given to an Overseer, an official appointed annually by members of the parish governing body.

Although he was unpaid the Overseer had considerable power and his job was to provide money or bread; supervise the parish poorhouse; provide work for adult members of the village; apprentice poor children and find them work, and suppress and punish vagabonds and beggars.

Under the Relief of the Poor Act 1601 that finally received official assent in 1604, every parish in England became self-governing, responsible for its own people and the Overseer was also given power to raise money by use of the Poor Rate, an early form of income tax that was based on the ability of each household to pay. This eventually evolved into a property tax or rate, based on the value of properties in the village,

Esholt is a village full of beautiful
'chocolate box' cottages

although it was normally the tenant rather than the landlord who paid, with a summons to appear before the local magistrate the usual penalty for failure to pay.

The Overseer of Esholt also kept account books which recorded every item spent or collected and these provide some fascinating and tragic tales of what life was like in the village. For example, in June 1815, the Overseer of that year, Matthew Mitchell, had nothing to record, yet six months later he handed over two shillings (10p) a week for forty-one weeks to a militia-man's wife, which indicates she needed financial support because her husband was with the army of the Duke of Wellington fighting the French forces of Napoleon.

Mitchell's successor, Peter Grimshaw, is recorded as having "provided William Hartley with shirt, coat, rent, britches and shoes." In 1821-22 Mr Hartley was before the Overseer again and this time he was given three yards of cloth at one-shilling and two pence (6p) a yard to make clothing; and a year later received another shirt. Two years later the accounts of 1825 showed him needing shoes, shirt, coat, waistcoat and britches.

Dealing with tragedy too was also part of the responsibility of the Overseer and Peter Grimshaw entered in his book for 1823-4: "Ann Picker's child burnt, 4 shillings (20p); burying Ann Picker's child, 6 shillings (30p)."

Twenty years later Overseer Thomas Denby entered the account book on October 1, that he had provided 3d (1p) for half a pound of soap for Sarah Johnson. On October 17 he doled out a shilling (5p) for "attending Sarah Johnson," and on October 24 for buying Sarah a half pound of soap again. The tragic entry, however, came on November 2, with: "expenses for Sarah Johnson's funeral £2.2s.2½ (£2.12p).

A few weeks later and the budget of the Overseer improved when Dendy recorded: "Received from the sale of Sarah Johnson's effects £4.0s.4½d (£4.01p)."

A further entry with more than a hint of sadness was a note pinned inside the accounts which read: "This is to certify that John Bell is laid dead at the infirmary and his relations cannot afford to bury him, therefore be kind enough to allow the money for the funeral. A.E. Bell, Monday, December 7, 1847." The Overseer at that time was Peter Grimshaw again, who evidently did sterling work in Esholt, for he entered in the book: "John Bell's funeral, £1"

There is little doubt that approaching the Overseer was usually the last desperate act for most villagers and the money and goods doled out would not have been given without a good deal in inquiry into the personal circumstances of those applying for relief. History, however, fails to record what happened to the good folk of Esholt whose request for help was refused!

Above: Husbands or sons fighting the French forces of Napoleon caused great hardship for some Esholt families

The Naughty Nuns of Esholt

We have already seen that Esholt was once home to a priory that was authorised in 1172 by Pope Alexander III, but few villagers realise that some of this group of God's followers failed miserably to be as holy as the church would have expected. For history shows us that there was certainly a group of naughty nuns within the walls of St Mary and St Leonard nunnery in Esholt and in 1303 the prioress Juliana de Wood-hall, who had held the post for only three years, offered to resign after it was discovered that one of the nuns, Beatrice de Hawkesworth, was pregnant. Even worse was the disclosure that the offender was the widow of Walter Hawkesworth, a known villain, albeit a member of the local gentry, who had a conviction for stealing a deer from his neighbour.

This travesty of holy orders was only the tip of the Esholt iceberg for records show that the Archbishop of York, William Greenfield, who had initially refused to accept the resignation of prioress Woodhall until he had the full facts, later wrote to her and ordered her to remove within six days all women boarders over twelve years of age and forbade her to admit any more without special licence. Only twenty-four hours earlier he had confirmed the election of Isabella de Calverley as Woodhall's successor.

Despite a change of prioress it seems the morals of some of the nuns at Esholt continued to take a downward turn and thirty years after the first outbreak of randy sisters there were other incidents that prompted the then Archbishop of York, William Melton, to order Dr. Clyf, his Vicar-General, to visit Esholt to see for himself what was happening. Dr. Clyf's findings prompted the archbishop to send a list of formal church injunctions that ordered her to provide sufficient locks and keys for the cloister doors which were to be locked securely each night and not opened again until seven o'clock the following morning in winter and six in the summer. The Archbishop also ordered all nuns to obey the orders of the prioress and observe church rules as they had sworn to do when they took to holy orders and furthermore ordered the prioress should "suffer no ale-house to be kept within the precinct of the gates". It seemed that the nuns brewed more ale in the priory than they needed for their personal use (ale having a greater use in those times than water with meals) and normally sold the surplus.

A further order stated: "No manner of persons was

to be allowed to lie or lodged within the cloister" and that "no sister was to go out of the precinct of the monastery without some just cause."

One nun, Joanna Hutton, aged 30, was discovered to have "brought forth a child of her bed begotten," which had caused a great scandal and the Archbishop sent an order that although he was "willinge to reforme the same horrible crime" the prioress was to lock her away for two years on a diet of bread and ale only every Wednesday and Friday and abstain from all "flesh, fish, butter, eggs, cheese and milk". Each Friday Hutton was also ordered to do penance in the presence of the other sisters in a manner laid down by the prioress. We can only speculate on what the punishment each Friday was, and on what happened to Hutton's baby. When Esholt priory was dissolved in 1540 only ten nuns remained.

Nun contemplating, from a painting by 19th century German artist G.A. Kuntz

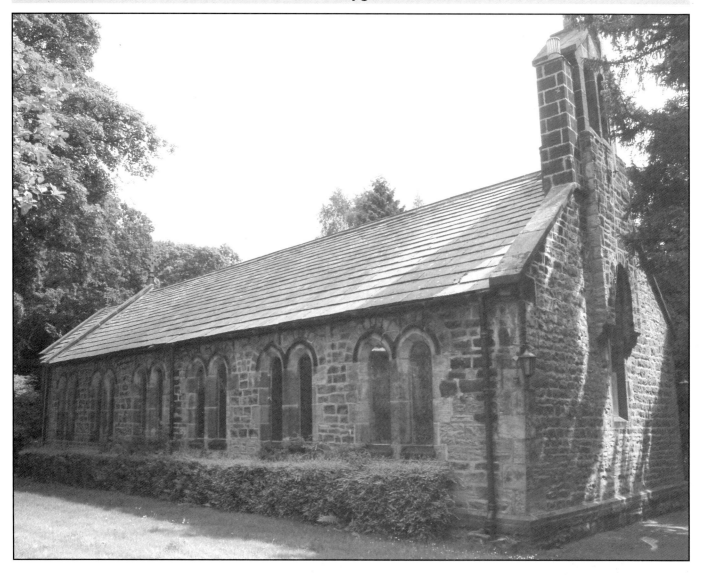

St Paul's Church, Esholt, was once the private chapel of William Rookes Crompton Stansfield.
The building is familiar to long time viewers of Emmerdale as it was once used for exterior location filming

Esholt Church

St Paul's Church was built in 1839 by William Rookes Crompton Stansfield as a private chapel, but on September 2, 1853, the building, originally without a chancel, was consecrated by the Right Reverend Charles Thomas Langley, the Bishop of Ripon, for use as a public place of worship. It became a parish church in 1856.

The cost of building the church was £800, the equivalent today of about £80,000.

It was 1895 before St Paul's had a chancel added at a cost of £259, a personal gift from the three Misses Crompton-Stansfield, patrons of the church, in memory of their father, Major General William Crompton-Stansfield and their mother Frances. The church also houses a pulpit with carved oak panels which are thought to date from the 16th century and new pews were added in 1928 after cash was raised by public subscription.

On June 1, 1983, the parish was merged with that of nearby St Oswald's in Guiseley, to become formally the Parish of Guiseley with Esholt. The link with St Oswald's is of interest to lovers of Bronte literature for it was here that Patrick Bronte and Maria Branwell, the parents of the three famous authors, Charlotte, Emily and Anne, were married on Monday, December 29, 1812.

The entrance porch to Esholt Church

The well proportioned and attractive interior of St Paul's Church, Esholt, which was also once used as a location for Emmerdale

Esholt Waste and Water

Between 1801 and 1851 the population of the nearby town of Bradford increased from 13,500 residents to more than 100,000 because of the huge growth in the textile industry. Naturally, as with such a large population growth, the problems of public health manifested itself and since the law was lax in the matter of sewage control and clean water, diseases such as typhus, smallpox and scarlet fever was soon rampant in the area, and cholera too claimed some lives.

Human waste and the waste from mills and factories was dumped into local water courses, or becks, which eventually found its was into the River Aire that runs close to Esholt and within a couple of hundred yards of Esholt Hall.

The incredible pollution of the Aire, once a lovely little river meandering through meadows and woodland, was becoming a major cause for concern in the area, and in February, 1869, William Stansfield of Esholt Hall could stand the smell no longer and decided it was time for action. He was granted an interim injunction against Bradford Corporation which ordered city fathers to clean up its act and improve the sewage system. The Corporation let fly a few salvoes of its own at Stansfield, claiming, probably with some justification, that he too was partly responsible for the river's pollution since his own mills in the Esholt district also poured waste from cleaning and dyeing into the Aire.

The Corporation had already realised that theirs was a growing problem for they had started work in 1862 on a new sewage works, though by the time of Stansfield's' complaint the work was far from complete. To try and sort the conundrum the Corporation proposed an early form of a public and private partnership when they suggested building a new sewage works that could be leased to a private company to operate. The idea was that the firm could provide the sewage disposal service free for three years and in return make money from selling a purified fertiliser as a by-product of the works. Alas, the scheme failed as the sewage was too rich in chemicals and grease to be used as a fertiliser. Shortly afterwards a new court injunction was granted to Stansfield which prohibited any further discharge into the waterways.

As Bradford's population continued to grow, waste disposal problems became more acute and the wrangle between the Corporation and the Stansfield family also continued. By 1897 the status of becoming a city instead of a town made the Corporation more assertive and when the city boundaries were extended in 1899 the decided, in a strange twist of fate, that the most suitable site for a new sewage works would be on the Esholt estate! The legal wrangle went on for a further seven years but in the end the whole of the Esholt estate was sold to the city fathers for a mere quarter of a million pounds.

Once the sale had been completed the construction of a new sewage works started and eventually a three miles long tunnel was built at enormous cost which connected the existing facilities at Frizinghall and Esholt. It took until 1920 before the project was complete and in 1926 the Esholt sewage works took over completely and Fitzinghall was closed.

The Esholt facility had its own laboratory and team of scientists who worked on the earlier problem of ex-

Esholt Hall as it looks today, still a magnificent mansion and a wonderful example of a classic regency building. Now owned by Yorkshire Water it is used as a conference centre, but visitors can still get an overall feeling of what life must have been like here two centuries ago

Left: A 19th century water-colour painting of Esholt Hall which still hangs inside the building

Below: Esholt Water Works

tracting grease from the waste and the result was the emergence of a number of products that were sold commercially, including paint and polish. Ironically, paint from one of the by-products was even used to paint Esholt Hall!

By 1949 the Esholt plant proved conclusively that the old adage 'where there's muck there's brass' is true, for income from the works was covering all costs and indeed was making a healthy profit for the council. It was a unique situation that the very estate that had been at the centre of a political row for thirty years was now giving its one time adversary the means of being possibly the only Corporation in the county making a profit from sewage.

Today Esholt Hall and its grounds is owned and operated by Yorkshire Water and the hall is now used as a conference centre with plans afoot to develop much of the previous industrial land into a research and development-led technology business park.

Esholt Hall itself remains the centrepiece of this ambitious plan, with listed buildings converted into offices and more buildings in the immediate vicinity of the hall also being earmarked for conversion. The hall, which has been restored, offers twenty-four conference and function rooms that are available for private dinner parties and weddings, and it is a singular example of how the past can still be preserved in a sensitive way while catering for the needs of today.

Esholt Hall is undoubtedly a Yorkshire treasure that may not be as splendid as some halls in the country but is one that should be preserved for future generations.

A 19th century painting of the stairway in Esholt Hall

Above: The stairway in Esholt Hall as it looks today.

Right: The old stables gateway at Esholt.

Once providing accommodation for the Stansfield family's horses, the old stables at Esholt Hall have now been converted into warm, comfortable homes and offices

Esholt and Emmerdale

There is little doubt that Esholt must be one of the most recognised villages in the world thanks to its use as the location between 1976 and 1998 for Emmerdale. Known for years as 'Beckindale' in the TV series it continues to attract thousands of visitors a year despite the fact that pressure of increased filming made it necessary for the TV company to abandon it in favour of a new, purpose built facsimile set in the grounds of the private Harewood estate several miles away.

The Woolpack and the Post Office still attract most visitors as they continue to be the only actual locations that operate as on-going businesses that can be visited.

A closed set rule at Harewood has been beneficial to Esholt because as one local said: "If the location at Harewood was open to the public then, of course, they would go there rather than to Esholt. But since the village is the only place where they can get the atmosphere and feel of Emmerdale then the tourists still come, which is good news for local businesses in and around Esholt."

The Home farm of the series, always home to Emmerdale's richest family, is based on a real life Home farm that dates back to 1691which still exists on the Esholt estate, though many of the original buildings are now derelict.

Other properties within a few miles of the village were also used as locations but it is undoubtedly Esholt itself that has been the star of the show for more than three decades, and it is remarkable that despite the onslaught of tourism over the decades the village remains such a beautiful and historically important place.

Above: The famous Post Office in Esholt, known throughout the world at the home of the Windsor family in Emmerdale

Pear Tree Cottage, Esholt

Pear Tree Cottage

In many fictional TV series the names of houses or other buildings are changed, but in Esholt the names of many properties are the same as those in Emmerdale. Perhaps the most famous of these, after the pub and post noffice, is Pear Tree Cottage which stands next door to the Woolpack.

In the series too Pear Tree Cottage is the first in a row of houses and that is certainly the case in Esholt. Indeed the cottage proudly boasts a plaque above the front porch proclaiming its name for fans and the rest of the world to see!

So who lives in Pear Tree Cottage in Emmerdale and what is its fictional history?

Over the decades it has been a family home and was once owned by the powerful Tate dynasty. After the devastating storyline of Chris Tate who, finding he had a brain tumour and discovering his wife Charity was having an affair with her cousing Cane Dingle, committed suicide but left clues that suggested murder and pointing the finger at Charity, she had to move into Pear Tree Cottage after not being allowed to remain in Home Farm.

Here Charity lived with her other cousin Marlon for company. Marlon was depressed because his then wife, Trisha, had opted to go to India and he and Charity took to drinking too much with the inevitable one-night stand being the outcome.

After Tricia returned from her India jaunt she moved into Pear Tree Cottage with Marlon and Charity but, inevitably, the truth came out about Marlon's infidelity and Tricia left, afterwards being killed in a storm that swept Emmerdale.

Marlon, swept with grief, moved out of Pear Tree Cottage and moved into Wishing Well Cottage, the home of his uncle Zac Dingle.

Meanwhile, Charity Dingle continued to live in Pear Tree Cottage until she met the new 'sugar daddy' millionaire businessman Tom King and his family of four sons. Quick to know when she was onto a good thing Charity moved into the King's much more elaborate home and Pear Tree Cottage was rented to Charity's buxon cousin Chastity and local youngsters Katie Sugden and Danny Daggert.

The threesome remained in Pear Tree Cottage for several months until Tom King decided it would make an ideal office base for the King empire which was making its presence felt far and wide in and around Emmerdale. Thus Pear Tree Cottage became the headquarters for King and Sons, a use it has to this day.

In real life Pear Tree Cottage is the first cottage most visitors notice after looking at the Woolpack but, unfortunately for those wishing a closer look, it is a private home and not open to the public.

Emmerdale characters Marlon Dingle (Mark Charnock) and Chastity Dingle (Lucy Pargeter).

Real life licencees of The Woolpack in Esholt, are husband and wife team Richard and Nicki McGrath, seen here with a collection of Emmerdale cast pictures in the pub

The Woolpack

In Emmerdale there is no doubt that it is The Woolpack Inn that is the centre of every storyline, with villagers gathering at every opportunity to have a drink and a natter with their neighbours (or in some cases a punch-up!) and it has had many licencees over the years, the most famous of them being the deadly duo of Henry Wilks and Amos Brearley (played by Arthur Pentelow and Ronald Magill) who brought a brilliant deadpan humour to the programme. However, when Arthur Pentelow died his character had to be written out of the series, followed shortly afterwards by the retirement to Spain of Amos, having married Annie Sugden (Sheila Mercier) the show's matriarch.

The first Woolpack was the Falcon Inn in Arncliffe, a small village in north Yorkshire, but when filing of the outdoor scenes were moved to Esholt in 1976 the Commercial Inn was chosen as the new Woolpack.

The present Woolpack is on the purpose built Emmerdale village set on the Harewood Hall estate and is based on the Woolpack in Esholt. Despite this, however, it is to the genuine pub in Esholt that fans of the show enjoy visiting as this is the building they remember and love.

Today the licensees are Richard and Nicki McGrath who welcome Emmerdale fans from around the world who drop in and hope to see a famous face or two.

The interior of The Woolpack is smaller and different in its layout to the TV pub, but there is still a genuine Yorkshire welcome for visitors.

Top: Main Street, Esholt, with the Post Office seen on the right.

Right: Visitors from all over the world descend on the village all year round and love walking in the footsteps of the many famous Emmerdale characters who have trod these very roads and paths.

Main Street

Main Street in Esholt is just that - the main street of the village and is probably the most familiar location in Emmerdale. It is home to The Woolpack, the Post Office, and most of the cottage homes of the programme's main characters.

We have already discussed Pear Tree Cottage, but next door is the equally well known Woodbine Cottage where Edna Birch, the outwardly surly character who has high moral standards but a soft centre and her dog live. Over the years Edna, played by Shirley Stelfox, has taken in numerous lodgers, much to the chagrin of her neighbours, but despite being hurt time after time by people taking advantage of her Christian nature, Edna refuses to believe everyone is bad.

Next door to Woodbine Cottage is Tug Ghyll, which was once owned by Scott Windsor but these days is owned by the surprisingly ruthless Debbie Dingle (Charley Webb), who also runs the Emmerdale garage.

Main Street is also the setting for the Grange Bed and Breakfast which is located in Emmerdale just across the road from the Post Office. Once owned by Alan Turner (who also once ran The Woolpack) the B & B has been the setting for some pretty strong storylines of intrigue, kidnap and murder. After a traumatic story of Turner being held at the mercy of his mentally unbalanced daughter Steph (played by Lorraine Chase) and the killing of his equally neurotic son Terrence (played by Nick Brimble), Alan sold the B & B to shapely Australian Louise Appleton (played by Emily Symons, a genuine Australian) and Terry Woods (played by Scotsman Billy Hartman).

On the opposite side of Main Street, next door to the Post Office, is Keepers Cottage, where Betty Eagleton (Paula Tilbrook) lives. Betty is the village gossip who, like Edna Birch, has a heart of gold, and she has played host to many of the village people who have fallen on hard times either financially or emotionally, including Alan Turner, to whom she offered a home following his traumatic experiences. Latterly she has been co-habiting with Sandy Thomas, (played admirably by Freddie Jones) father of the village vicar Ashley Thomas. Of course her most famous partner was loveable rogue Seth Armstrong (Stan Richards), the local gamekeeper, who died while on an overseas trip.

Next to Betty's cottage is Victoria Cottage, once the home of newly-weds Marlon Dingle and Tricia Stokes. Following the breakup of their marriage, and Tricia's subsequent death following a storm in Emmerdale, the cottage was rented to the Marsdens's, before being bought by Matthew King who rented it to timid Emily Kirk and Paul Lambert, gay son of co-owner of the Woolpack, Val Lambert. After Emily left the cottage Paul's father Rodney (Patrick Mower) moved in. The saga continues...

Also available

If you have enjoyed reading this book then you may also wish to read

Holmfirth
A Bygone Era

By Peter Riley

32pp, illustrated. Only £3.

This title offers fans of the popular BBC TV comedy series *Last of the Summer Wine*
the opportunity to learn all about the town that is used as its main location.
Over the past 36 years Holmfirth has boomed as a tourist centre thanks to the programme which is now
the world's longest running comedy series, but there is far more to Holmfirth than Summer Wine. It has
had a long and varied existence as the home of Bamforth's who produced all those saucy postcards
everyone has seen at British holiday resorts; it was also one of Britain's earliest film centres, with movies
being made in and around this lovely town almost a century ago. It has also suffered several devastating
floods. Despite all this, however, the town and surrounding area have remained timeless and beautiful.

ISBN: 978-1-874712-72-5

**Order through any good bookseller or buy online direct from the publisher on
www.pdriley.co.uk**